# Preventive Vet
# 101 ESSENTIAL TIPS
## Dog Health & Safety

DR. JASON NICHOLAS
Illustrated by Chuck Gonzales

PREVENTIVE VET
Portland, OR

The material in this book is based on the author's professional opinion and experience; it is supplied here for general informational purposes only. This material is not meant to take the place of an established veterinarian-client-patient relationship. For your pet's health and safety, please consult with your veterinarian for individualized care and prior to making any medical decisions regarding your pet's health.

First published 2013.
Second edition published 2016.

ISBN: 978-0-9883781-6-2

Book cover and interior design by
Robin Walker, The YGS Group

Illustrations by Chuck Gonzales

Printed in North America.

PREVENTIVE VET

# CONTENTS

# INTRODUCTION

You've got a new dog! Fun! And you've likely got your hands full now, too. And so much to learn! But you don't have time to read a whole "puppy owner's manual" or scour the web for everything you need to know. Worry not, 101 Essential Tips boils it down for you and provides reliable, essential dog care information in short, easy-to-read tips—so you can learn a few things during cuddle time, between play sessions, or even when you finally get some peace and quiet on the toilet. (Hey, I'm not too proud. I don't mind if you read it in the bathroom, I just want you to know this stuff!)

These are the tips and insights I've gathered over my years of practice and from talking with other vets and dog lovers, not to mention my own experiences of having dogs (including having dogs while also having kids, cats, and an otherwise busy life, too). These tips will help you keep your dog—and your credit card—out of the ER, and they'll help you have a better overall life together, as well.

Of course, it's just not possible to cover every aspect of each of these topics in a short tip format. But don't worry, your vet is there to help, and I'm not going to leave you "hanging" either—this book also gives you exclusive access to the "Book Extras" section on our website, for when you want to dive into a topic in more detail.

One last note: 101 Essential Tips isn't just for first-time dog owners! Even if you've grown up with dog, or had several as an adult, every dog and every situation is different and there's always something new to learn. And given all that's at stake, it's far better for you to learn these things the easy way now from my experience and the experiences of others, than to do so "the hard way" later. So, dig in and may you and your new pup have many wonderful, healthful, happy years together! Enjoy!

Dr. Jason Nicholas

# BONUS ONLINE CONTENT

**BOOK EXTRAS**

## Extra Extra!
## Learn More About It!

Don't miss Book Extras, where you get exclusive access to additional content, videos, downloads, and … contests!

Go to *PreventiveVet.com/Book-Extras*, enter this code: *3HS-T2F6-8D* to unlock this free bonus section.

**WANT $250 TO SPEND AT YOUR VET?**
Enter our contest for your chance to win.
USE CODE: *3HS-T2F6-8D*
PreventiveVet.com/Book-Extras

# CHAPTER 1

# Dogs Will Eat Just About Anything!

# 1 When sharing isn't caring

The foods we eat are often too rich, spicy, or varied for our dogs (and some are even poisonous to them!). Table scraps, and the "love" you think you're sharing, can easily land your pup in the hospital with a serious, expensive, and potentially fatal digestive problem. To dogs, the act of getting a treat is what's most important, so opt for giving them a dog treat instead of your food. Feeding table scraps also encourages begging—which may be cute when your dog is a pup, but will grow old well before they do!

**Conan** an overweight, 5-year-old Shih Tzu, had to spend five days in the Animal ICU recovering from a severe and painful case of pancreatitis after he got some prime rib leftovers as a special treat. Though his hospitalization and treatment cost his owners over $3,000, they felt guilty about his condition and were ecstatic to have their beloved Conan feeling better. From the day of his discharge they worked with their veterinarian to get Conan back to a more ideal body condition and vowed to express their love for him with additional walks and cuddles, not food.

## 2 Rawhides and pig ears: Buyer beware

If your dog is a "chewer," these treats will probably be fine. But if your dog is a "gulper" or "inhaler" these treats will be neither safe nor effective. They'll be unsafe because large chunks of these treats can cause distress and a potentially fatal obstruction of your pup's digestive or respiratory systems when swallowed or inhaled. And they'll be ineffective because if your dog isn't thoroughly chewing them, they aren't getting any of the advertised teeth-cleaning benefits anyway. Monitor closely to find out which group your pup falls into and then use (or don't) accordingly, and always under supervision.

*Note: Because of their source and production process, pig ears and rawhides can commonly become contaminated with disease-causing Salmonella bacteria, or even potentially concerning processing chemicals, like formaldehyde and ammonium-containing compounds. If used, select only products from reputable manufacturers and avoid chews from open-air "bulk bins."*

## 3 Deer antlers—'doe' not give these to your dog!

You've probably seen deer and elk antlers touted as all-natural, sustainably harvested, eco-friendly, amazing chews for dogs. Sadly though, if you ask most vets and veterinary dentists, you're likely to hear plenty of stories of dogs that suffered painful (and expensive) tooth fractures from chewing on antlers! It's their hardness that makes them so long-lasting—heck they can withstand the force of a collision with another antler in battle—but it's that same hardness that causes countless teeth to fracture each year. And these teeth require either removal or repair (root canal), or they'll be a chronic source of pain and could also act as an entryway for bacteria into your dog's tooth root and general bloodstream. I highly recommend that you keep your dog away from antlers; there are far safer things for your dog to chew on. And those icy treats: ice cubes. They break teeth, too! Check out Book Extras for some better chew options and teething tips for young pups.

## 4 Chocolate—do you know everything you need to?

Though many dog owners are seemingly aware of its potentially life-threatening danger, chocolate toxicity remains one of the most common poisonings seen at veterinary hospitals and called into pet poison control hotlines. While these cases happen year-round, they always escalate around the holidays, so take extra care around these times of the year. And since chocolates with higher cocoa content (i.e., "darker") are more dangerous, be especially careful when baking with bittersweet or baker's chocolate, as they contain the most theobromine, which is related to caffeine and is the thing that causes the most problems in dogs. If your dog ever eats chocolate (including cocoa mulch in the garden—Tip #40), call your veterinarian, Animal ER, or a pet poison control hotline immediately. However, if your dog is already anxious, panting, or having seizures, bring them immediately for veterinary care.

## 5 Macadamia nuts can stop your dog in their tracks ... temporarily

Given their high levels of "healthy fats" and the vitamin and mineral "punch" they pack for people, macadamia nuts are no longer just a holiday treat or nice present from someone returning from a Hawaiian vacation. However, these little nutritional powerhouses should *not* be shared with your pooch! Macadamia nut toxicity can cause stumbling, tremors and high fever in dogs, and it can even cause their back legs to stop working properly. Thankfully, these toxic effects are usually temporary and resolve on their own or with minimal supportive care at the vet. If the macadamias are covered in chocolate, though ... that's a whole different beast!

## 6 No bones about it! Giving your dog a bone comes with great risk.

All bones, whether cooked or raw, beef, pork, or chicken, have the potential to break your dog's teeth and/or obstruct, irritate, or puncture their digestive tract. Any of these issues will be painful and costly, and many can land your dog on the dental or surgery table. There are safer options to satisfy your dog's natural desire for chewing (including plenty of chew toys with enough "give"), and better ways to care for their teeth, too.

**Maximus** a 4-year-old English Mastiff, occasionally got marrow bones as a treat. One day he broke a tooth while chewing on one. The fractured tooth was discovered only when he was brought to his vet two days later because he was sleeping more and not eating. Because the broken tooth was painful, and was also at increased risk of becoming infected, his owners were given the choice of having it removed by their vet or taking Maximus to a veterinary dentist for a root canal. They elected to have the broken tooth removed and forever swore off giving Maximus bones as treats.

## 7 Garlic—it's not just vampires that should steer clear!

Though most dogs won't voluntarily gobble down handfuls of chives, onion, garlic, or leeks, plenty will be more than happy to steal your onion rings, garlic bread, or chive mashed potatoes the second you turn your back! Should your dog do so, it won't just be a tasty side dish you'll be losing, it may also cost you several hours, thousands of dollars, and potentially even your dog's life. That's because these common culinary staples—all plants belonging to the *Allium* genus—contain compounds that will destroy a dog's red blood cells. The condition, known as hemolytic anemia, is dangerous and debilitating, and can be fatal without—and sometimes even with—treatment. This is the same type of anemia that can result from penny ingestion (Tip #12). And be careful, too, with any broths you may buy or make to help tempt your dog's appetite or thirst, as onions and garlic, either fresh or in their powdered form, are commonly used in broth recipes!

## 8 'Grape Expectations'

Eating even a small number of grapes (or raisins or currants) may be enough to cause a devastating case of acute kidney failure in your dog. Not every dog is affected by this poisoning, and it's not even known yet what the exact toxin is. Given the severity of kidney failure in affected dogs though, it's best to avoid *any* exposure to these common fruits and snacks. And keep in mind that each of these fruits are also found in a variety of common products—including trail mix, breads, bagels, and cookies. They're also a common snack given to toddlers, and therefore often end up on the floor or being fed directly to dogs by children who love to share.

## 9 Xylitol—OK for people, REALLY bad for dogs!

Xylitol is an all-natural sugar substitute made from birch trees, corn cobs, and other plant-based sources. It's gaining in popularity because of its anti-cavity properties, and benefits for diabetic people, and those on a "keto," "Paleo," or "low-carb" diets. However, xylitol is extremely dangerous to dogs! Even a small amount can be fatal by dropping your dog's blood sugar or destroying their liver. Xylitol is often found in sugar-free gum, mints, chewable vitamins, toothpaste (Tip #71), mouthwash, baked goods, and many other popular products—including some nut and peanut butters. Carefully read ingredient labels and keep all sources of xylitol well out of your dog's reach. Check out Book Extras for a list of more than 700 products that contain xylitol—you'll be surprised by how many foods and common household products contain this ingredient!

## 10 Bakers beware!

Your dog's stomach is an ideal proofing oven for bread, pizza, and other doughs containing yeast, so you need to keep these doughs well out of their reach. If your dog were to eat such dough, the yeast would become "active" in their warm stomach, causing the dough to "rise." The result would be a painful and dangerous buildup of gas and alcohol that could lead to stomach bloat (Tip #76), digestive obstruction, alcohol poisoning, and even death. Don't give your dog the opportunity. Leave all yeast dough to rise safely on an elevated shelf, in the microwave, or in the oven—not on the kitchen counter or table within your dog's reach (Tip #25). If you see your dog eat dough that contains yeast, immediately give them ice water to drink and contact your veterinarian or Animal ER for further advice.

## 11 These two common items can 'burn a hole' in your dog … and your wallet

Batteries are everywhere—from remote controls and children's toys to holiday ornaments and even hearing aids, which are covered in (tasty to dogs) earwax! If your dog swallows a battery, especially one of the disc or button-type batteries, it can get stuck and cause severe burns anywhere along their digestive tract. These types of burns often lead to expensive surgery and a prolonged hospital stay, or worse. If your pup has a habit of chewing or scavenging (and many dogs do!), be extra careful about where you leave your batteries and battery-powered devices.

Magnets are often swallowed by dogs, too. And when more than one is swallowed, the magnets can attract each other, pinching the dog's intestines between them, and cutting off the blood supply. This can result in a hole in their digestive tract, and leakage of food and bacteria from their gut. The resulting "peritonitis" will be painful and can be fatal if your pup isn't treated in time. Keep all magnets—including your children's magnetic toys and your prized collection of fridge magnets—picked up and well out of your dog's reach.

## 12 A $1,000 penny

Should your dog ever eat a penny—which, believe it or not, many have done—the year in which the penny was minted will determine if their "hunger for money" will cost you just that 1 cent, or several hundred to thousands of dollars. Pennies minted after 1982 are 97% zinc, an element that, when eaten, causes not only significant stomach irritation, but also severe breakdown of your dog's red blood cells. This breakdown of red cells, known as hemolytic anemia, causes lethargy and weakness, and is fatal if not treated. So, as the old adage goes find a penny, PICK IT UP! Doing so will improve your luck—and your dog's.

## 13 To your dog, that beautifully wrapped gift has their name on it

Wrapping paper, tape, and ribbon are no match for a dog hot on the scent of a box of chocolates or some other enticingly smelly gift. Depending on their breed and the shape of their head, a dog's sense of smell can be 10,000 to 100,000 times more sensitive than that of a person! So no amount of wrapping will block the scent from reaching their nose—or stop their paws or teeth. Be careful what you leave within your dog's reach, and be sure that houseguests ... including Santa, the Easter Bunny, and even Cupid—exercise the same caution.

## 14 What eats more socks than a dryer?

Dogs! Your pup loves how you smell, so they might be tempted to play with your dirty laundry when you're not around. If that play turns into chewing … nom, nom, nom … and swallowing then they're in trouble. Many a dollar has been spent removing socks, towels, underwear, and other garments from the stomachs and intestinal tracts of dogs. Put all dirty laundry in closed hampers and keep your dog out of the laundry room. Don't forget about children's rooms, too. And be extra cautious with baby and toddler clothes, which are often stained with all kinds of enticing food (and other) splatters. Oh, and speaking of laundry … be sure to keep bleach, laundry detergent pods, and dryer sheets well out of your dog's reach, too.

## 15 Hide the 'Kitty Crunchers'

"Kitty Crunchers," "Kitty Roca," or just plain old "cat poop." Whatever you call it, your dog calls it "DELICIOUS!" Unfortunately, these litter box snacks are not at all kind to your dog's digestive system—and the results won't be kind to your carpets either. Prevent your dog's access by keeping litter boxes behind baby gates or partially cracked doors (prevent full opening with an eye-hook or "door strap"). Your cat will appreciate this, too! And even if you don't have a cat, if you ever bring your dog to visit someone who does, be sure to keep this tip in mind.

## 16 Vaping: New ways for dogs to get into old problems

As more people switch from smoking to vaping, dogs are exposed to new ways to get into trouble. Dogs seemingly love to steal and chomp down on eCigs, vape pens, and the refill cartridges for either. Not only do these contain dangerously high concentrations of compounds that can be harmful to dogs—like nicotine, and THC, but the devices are also battery powered. Even though they're not button batteries (Tip #11), the rechargeable lithium batteries these devices are often powered by can still cause some pretty serious problems for dogs that bite down on them! And keep in mind that, just like secondhand smoke, secondhand vapor can also cause breathing problems for dogs, especially those with existing respiratory conditions, like chronic bronchitis or collapsing trachea.

## 17 It's OK for dogs to eat grass; just don't let them eat 'weed'

An alarming number of dogs wind up at the vet suffering from marijuana (THC) toxicity—especially from "edibles!" If you keep weed in your home, or if somebody brings it over, in whatever form, be careful to keep it well out of your dog's reach. If your dog gets into it, don't let them "sleep it off." Bring them in for the care they need. Don't worry, we vets aren't interested in "ratting" you out. We just need the info to best care for your dog. PS: Cannabidiols (CBD) may actually have some medical benefits for dogs, and without the "high" of its psychoactive cousin, THC. This is an area of ongoing research and currently little regulation though. Check out Book Extras for more on this popular topic.

## 18 Antifreeze—a tasty danger!

Most antifreeze (or engine coolant) contains a compound called ethylene glycol—an extremely dangerous compound for dogs. Even just a few licks of ethylene glycol can cause a debilitating, potentially fatal case of acute kidney failure in a dog. Properly store all antifreeze containers, promptly clean up all spills and leaks, and strongly consider using a pet-safer,* propylene glycol-based antifreeze instead.

*No antifreeze is truly pet-safe, but propylene glycol-based products are far safer than those with ethylene glycol (even those with bittering agents added).*

## 19 NEVER induce vomiting unless and until you've spoken with a veterinarian

In some cases, and with some poisons or toxins, making your dog vomit is NOT the right thing to do. In these instances, vomiting can actually be more dangerous for your dog than the poison they've swallowed (e.g., burning again on the way back up through the esophagus, or getting into their lungs and causing pneumonia). With any poisoning emergency, call your veterinarian, Animal ER, or a dedicated pet poison control hotline before trying to make your dog vomit. They can let you know if making your dog vomit is safe and appropriate, and can help talk you through the procedure if needed.

## 20 Beware the expanding blob ... of glue

Gorilla Glue® and other polyurethane glues are dangerous for dogs—and tempting, too! Dogs are attracted to these glues by their sweet smell and taste. Eating or licking even a small amount can result in a big problem ... a stomach obstruction that will require surgery to remove. The glue reacts to the acid and liquids in the dog's stomach, quickly expanding and hardening into a firm mass that they can't vomit or "pass." The rock-hard "glue masses" that are removed from dogs have typically expanded to fill the entire inside space of the stomach! They frequently form a perfect (though dangerous and debilitating) cast of the stomach that needs to be carefully "peeled away" from the sensitive stomach lining during surgery. Be sure to keep these glues well out of your pup's reach and clean up any spills after using them. To see a time-lapse video simulation of a dog's stomach after eating glue, check out Book Extras. It's not gross, we promise ... we use a see-through balloon, not an actual stomach.

**Tyson & Sitka** 3-year-old Boxer, Tyson, and Sitka, a 5-year-old Siberian Husky, panicked in their apartment when their owner accidentally locked herself out one day. In their excited state, they bumped into a shelf in the laundry room, knocking over a few of the items on the shelf—one of which happened to be a bottle of Gorilla Glue® The dogs made quick work of that bottle, and soon after their mom got herself back into her apartment, she had to head right back out again for an unplanned trip to the vet. Both dogs needed surgery to remove the hardened mass of glue that had formed in their stomachs. Tyson's was "basketball-sized," while Sitka's was "softball-sized." The surgeries set mom back more than $2,000, and the stress of the day's events likely set her back a few years of her life!

## 21 Prevent the 'All-You-Can-Eat Buffet'

Given the opportunity, many dogs will eagerly gorge themselves on their kibble—they don't really have an "off switch." By properly storing your dog's kibble supply behind a closet door, in a cabinet, or in a very secure storage bin, you'll prevent a painful and serious emergency called "food bloat" (not to be confused with GDV/Bloat—Tip #76). And keep this hazard in mind when taking your dog in the car on a vacation, too. Preventing their access to the bag of food you're likely traveling with is yet another reason for you to properly restrain your dog during travel (Tip #67: Travel safety, and Tip #28: Suffocation).

Marley a 1-year-old Labrador Retriever, decided one night that his hunger couldn't wait for breakfast. He helped himself to the bag of dry food his owners stored next to his food bowl, eating about half its contents while his owners slept. He was rushed to the Animal ER when his owners awoke to find him groaning in pain and laying on his side. He immediately felt better after stomach pumping and other hospital care, but his midnight buffet cost his parents $1,200 (not including a replacement bag of dog food!). They are now careful to keep his food in an airtight, "Marley-proof" container, which they keep behind the closed kitchen pantry door.

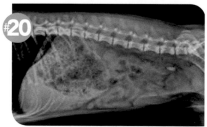

# CHAPTER 1 BONUS ONLINE CONTENT

*Enter **tip#** below at PreventiveVet.com/Book-Extras to access this information.*

**DON'T PUNISH THE PANCREAS:** Find out what a pancreas is and why it gets "angry." (#1)

**3 SIMPLE STEPS TO "CHEWSING" CHEWS:** How-tos for buying safer chews and chew toys. (#3)

**LUCY'S STORY:** See why she didn't win the battle with homemade zucchini bread. (#9)

**COMMON HOUSEHOLD PRODUCTS:** Check out a list of over 700 products that contain xylitol to make sure that you keep them out of reach of your dog. (#9)

**BUTTON BATTERIES BURN:** See a video of these batteries burning through ham and how quickly it can happen if they're swallowed by a dog or child. (#11)

**THE DANGER IS EVEN WORSE:** Find out why antifreeze is now even more dangerous for dogs. (#18)

**SEE WHAT CAME OUT OF HER STOMACH:** Watch CNN's video story about a pup who swallowed Gorilla Glue® to see what they took out and how hard it is. Crazy! (#20)

**BOOK EXTRAS**

*Go to **PreventiveVet.com/Book-Extras**, enter this code: **3HS-T2F6-8D** to unlock this resource*

Preventive Vet

# CHAPTER 2

# Safety In & Around The Home

## 22 Institute a 'closed-door policy' for houseguests

Though they don't do it on purpose, houseguests often bring any number of pet poisons and other hazards into your home in their suitcases, toiletry kits, purses, and jackets. Keeping those items off the floor and asking your guests to close the doors to their bedroom and bathroom will go a long way to keeping your pup safe and healthy.

**Shelby** an inquisitive 10-month-old Labrador Retriever puppy, needed an endoscopic procedure to remove the underwear she had eaten from the luggage of the aunt who was visiting for the holidays. As many overnight visitors will do, the aunt put her dirty clothes in her empty suitcase, which sat on the floor in the guestroom. Shelby's dietary adventures cost her family more than $800 and almost ruined their holiday plans. Now the door to the guestroom stays closed whenever visitors come to stay, and Shelby's family is careful to keep their own dirty laundry in a covered hamper in the laundry room.

## 23 Provide a 'safe space' in your home

This one precaution can prevent poisonings, cases of vomiting and diarrhea, bites to children, and a host of other problems. It's best to get your pup comfortable in this area when they're young and reacquaint them to it often and well in advance of any likely stressful event.

This area can be their crate or any pet-proofed quiet room that's off limits to houseguests and children— think of it as a low-stress sanctuary for your pup in your (likely) often-chaotic household. Having this space is particularly important around the holidays, during parties, when you have overnight visitors, during renovations, and when you bring a new baby or pet into your home.

## 24 Up, up, and away … for those treasure troves of hazards

Our bags often contain a variety of substances and products that are poisonous or otherwise harmful to our dogs. Hanging your gym bag, backpack, or purse from the back of a chair or from a doorknob really isn't safe enough, and neither is leaving them on a couch, table, or countertop. Getting in the habit of hanging all bags on wall hooks, coat racks, or behind closet doors is the best way to keep your pup truly safe.

And don't forget to ensure that all babysitters, houseguests, and other visitors take this simple precaution as well.

## 25 Counter surfing—the sport you don't want your dog excelling at

Given all the things that are often stored on nightstands and kitchen or bathroom countertops—it's best to discourage any desire your dog may have to "counter surf." Of course, that may be easier said than done, even with the use of crates and baby gates. After all, what good athlete doesn't like to strive for a new personal best?

So, play it extra safe and just don't store food and/or medications or supplements on your countertops or nightstands. Even if you think items are placed far enough from the edge—many dogs' reach is further than you might think, and plenty of small dogs are agile enough to get up on a counter (by climbing a chair, for example). Also, think about the family cat walking on the counter, knocking stuff off—perhaps Fluffy really is trying to poison your new pup!

## 26 When the '5-second' rule doesn't apply

Your dog's reflexes are faster than yours. This is why it is so important to get in the habit of dispensing *all* medications and supplements over a sink or bowl. Think about it—your pup won't have a chance to gobble up a pill that drops into a confined space (like the sink), but there's a good chance they'll beat you to the one that hits the floor! It's equally likely that they'll find the one that rolls under the couch before you do, too. Regardless of whether it's your pup's pills or yours, dispensing over a sink, tub, toilet, or bowl is easy to do and will help keep your dog safe from "medication poisoning"—which consistently tops the ASPCA's annual "Top 10 Pet Toxins" list.

**Hamish** a 6-year-old Scotty, didn't hesitate when several of his owner's prescription pills fell out of her hand and on to the floor while she was taking them one night before bed. Fortunately for Hamish, his owner didn't hesitate either and quickly called pet poison control. She got the information necessary to handle the problem at home and learned what to watch out for that would indicate that a trip to the Animal ER was necessary. Fortunately, Hamish was no worse for wear from his misadventures. And not wanting to tempt fate (or have another sleepless night), his mom now keeps all of her medications stored safely in the bathroom cabinet and always dispenses them over the sink.

## 27   Put the lid on 'dumpster diving'

To your dog, your household trash holds many tasty and tempting treats— very few of which are likely to be good for them. Using sturdy, covered trash cans and wastebaskets and keeping them safely out of reach behind cabinet or closet doors can save both of you a lot of pain and trouble—as well as a trip to the Animal ER. And don't forget about your outdoor trash and recycling bins, too!

Zelda a 12-year-old Jack Russell Terrier, had a habit of sneaking "extra snacks" from the trash. When she was a pup, her owners quickly learned to secure all their trash cans, and not to put anything too enticing in the smaller wastebaskets. Unfortunately, while Zelda's owners were traveling, their pet sitter discarded a tampon in the bathroom wastebasket.

It's difficult to know when Zelda got to it, but after three days of vomiting and lethargy she was brought to the vet suffering from shock. Her condition was critical, and Zelda suffered cardiac arrest and passed away while being prepped for emergency surgery.

There are many important lessons to be learned from Zelda's death. One of the more important ones though is that you, or whoever is dog sitting, should always consult your vet at the earliest signs of significant changes or problems. Waiting often prolongs suffering and can limit treatment options, as well.

# 28 Suffocation?
## Sadly, yes, and all too often!

Be it from a potato chip or other snack bag, the plastic liner from a cereal box, or even a bag of pet food or treats, far too many dogs die each year from suffocation after sticking their head into a bag that contains or used to contain food. It can take as little as 3 to 5 minutes for a dog to lose consciousness and succumb to the lack of oxygen—regardless of the size of the dog and even if someone is home. Keep your pup safe by cutting or tearing all bags twice—once along the bottom and once up a side, so the bag lays flat—before throwing it out. Check out Book Extras for more tips to help keep pets (and wildlife) safe from suffocation. There's also a sharable video and infographic to help spread the word.

**Finnegan** a 6-year-old Terrier mix, was always on the hunt for things to eat. His people were aware of this personality trait and did everything they could to keep "off-limit" foods out of his reach. One day they left an empty box of crackers on the kitchen counter, not thinking that it could cause a problem. Unfortunately, it did ... but it wasn't the digestive upset they normally worried about. Finnegan went for the crumbs in the box and suffocated in the bag lining the box. And it happened while his people were just upstairs! They were devastated when they found him, and had no idea that suffocation was even a "thing" they had to worry about. Finnegan's family was completely grief-stricken, and they still have a hard time coming to terms with the fear and pain their boy must have experienced in his final moments. They now cut and keep all bags out of reach of their other dogs, and do all they can to raise awareness of the dangers (and frequency) of pet suffocation.

## 29 These will light up your dog's life ... in a bad way!

For many puppies and anxious dogs, electrical cords and power cables are enticing chew toys! The shock your pup can get from chewing on these cords and cables won't only cause burns in their mouth, but it can also lead to seizures and fluid build-up in their lungs. Electric shock is painful, debilitating, expensive, and potentially fatal. And, as if that wasn't enough, a chewed cord can also spark a house fire. Safely position your pup's crate, bed, and food and water bowls away from any electrical cords and devices. And if you've got a chewer, try spraying some bitter spray on a cloth and rubbing down the cords, or use hard plastic cord covers to keep their inquisitive teeth off.

## 30 These shred more than just paper

Paper shredders pose serious risks to dogs. Curious or unfortunately placed tongues, tails, and ears can shred just as easily in some machines as paper does. Be safe—keep paper shredders off the floor or unplugged. If you do keep it plugged in, always keep it in the "off" position, never leave a paper shredder on "stand-by" or "automatic." Check out Book Extras for the eye-opening story of how the team at Tipp City Veterinary Hospital in Ohio freed a local office dog from the "bite" of a shredder.

## 31 Recline, sit back, relax— but with caution

An ill-placed paw, tail, or head can be (and sadly has been) crushed by the weight of a rocking chair or closing recliner. Always be mindful of where your pup is before sitting down, rocking, stretching out, or closing an extended footrest.

## 32 Door 'n' dash

Door-darting, -dashing or just plain bolting—whatever you call it—is a dangerous activity. Even though *you* know that opening a door is never an "open" invitation for your dog to bolt out, your dog may not. Any dog is likely to bolt if not trained, and some breeds with a strong prey drive (squirrel!) are even more apt to. Good training, sturdy baby gates, dog crates, and ensuring that you have a good grip on their leash or collar prior to opening any door are just some steps you can take that will go a long way toward preventing this risky behavior. And don't forget about the importance of yard fences for keeping a dog safe if they do ever successfully bolt out the door.

## 33 Fencing—not just an Olympic sport

Yard fences aren't only about keeping your dogs in; they keep other dogs (and wildlife) out, too. Both functions are important to prevent common emergencies like being hit by a car, wildlife or dog bites, poisonings, etc. Even if your dog doesn't spend time in your yard, a fence helps protect them if they ever bolt out the front door unexpectedly.

A word about electric dog fences: While they *may* do a decent job of preventing your dog from leaving your yard, they provide no protection against other dogs and animals coming in. For this, and many other reasons, a physical fence is preferable to an electric fence for safe, effective, and humane yard confinement.

## 34 Your pup and pools

Every year, too many puppies and young dogs die from avoidable drowning or "dry-drowning" accidents in their own backyard. If you (or your neighbors) have a pool, keep a close eye on your pup whenever they're outside and teach them how to find the stairs and safely get out of a pool should they jump or fall in. Sturdy pool covers or pool-perimeter fencing can help to keep your dog safe when you're not watching. But be aware that covers that aren't secured to the pool deck can actually make matters worse by trapping a fallen pup. Water surface alarms, doggie life jackets, puppy bumpers, and water safety ramps are great additional tools for backyard pool safety.

## 35 Life jackets for dogs? You bet!

Not all dogs are natural swimmers and some are more likely to panic or sink in the water. Even experienced swimmers can easily become exhausted and drown in the rough conditions or strong currents of a river, creek, lake, or ocean. Similarly, dogs that spend time on a kayak or boat, or riding the waves on a surfboard or stand-up paddle board are at risk of injury or drowning should they fall in. There are lots of doggie life jackets or PFDs (personal floatation devices) on the market. They're easy to use, and they can greatly improve your dog's safety in and around the water.

## 36   Make sure your catch-of-the-day is a fish—not your dog

Many owners have inadvertently "caught" their dog when they leave their fishing gear lying around or improperly stored. We in the veterinary emergency world have all seen dogs that have swallowed or been otherwise "caught" by fishing hooks while trying to lick off the remnants of bait or a recent catch. These injuries typically require sedation for removal of the hook, and some even require expensive and invasive surgery. Protect your dog and your wallet; always keep your tackle boxes and fishing rods well out of reach, whether out on the water or in your garage.

## 37   Garden of eatin'

Many common plants, flowers, and bulbs can be hazardous to your pup, and chances are that there's one (or several) in or around your home right now that could seriously sicken or even kill them. There are many signs of toxicity in dogs, ranging from drooling or mild skin irritation, all the way up to vomiting or collapse. Keep your dog out of your garden and train them to "leave it." In the event your pup does chew on or eat a plant, knowing what's safe and what's dangerous is an important step in safeguarding their health and safety. If there's any doubt, it's best to contact the experts at a pet poison control hotline, and to do so promptly. Taking a "wait-and-see" approach is never a good idea with any poisoning.

## 38 Yard work? Keep pup inside.

A hidden rock or stick can quickly become a dangerous projectile when struck by a lawnmower blade or a weed whacker. And if your pup's eye or head is in the path of that rock or stick, they're likely to suffer a painful injury. Don't take the chance. Keep your dog safely inside so they're not underfoot—or in harm's way—while you, or anyone else, is working with yard equipment. And always be mindful of grounds crews using motorized equipment when you and your pup are out and about.

## 39 Kill garden pests, not your dog

Most snail and slug baits contain a compound called metaldehyde, which is highly toxic not just to snails and slugs, but also to dogs. These baits are often formulated with molasses to attract garden pests, but the molasses also makes it more likely that your dog will be attracted, too! Once eaten, metaldehyde causes severe muscle tremors, which can lead to kidney failure and other problems that can be fatal. Try to use non-chemical types of snail and slug control, such as copper bands around your plants, crushed egg shells, or other DIY methods instead. If you must use chemicals, consider the pet-safer* option of an iron phosphate-based product.

*Even though iron phosphate-based products are safer than the metaldehyde-based slug and snail baits, they still pose a toxic risk to your pets if they were ever to ingest enough of it.*

## 40 A garden of chocolate?

More and more people are using cocoa mulch to help keep their gardens beautiful. You and/or your neighbors might even be among them. While cocoa mulch may be beneficial to your plants and flowers, its chocolate aroma may tempt your pup, and the theobromine content can make it dangerous for them. See Tip #4 for more on the dangers of cocoa and chocolate. And if you can't keep your dog out of your garden, then play it safe and keep the cocoa mulch out instead.

## 41 Some fungi are just no fun!

Not all mushrooms are edible, and certain ones in your yard or on hikes can be deadly. Of particular concern are those belonging to the *Amanita* genus—which can cause severe and rapid liver failure and is often fatal. Use caution on walks and hikes, and check your yard regularly to prevent your pup's exposure. To see what some of the more common poisonous mushrooms look like, check out Book Extras. And when in doubt about mushroom ID, try bringing a sample to your local garden center … someone there may just be able to help!

# 42 Sago palms—common, beautiful, and extremely dangerous!

Whether they're part of your outdoor landscaping or kept as houseplants, even a small nibble on a sago or other common cycad "palm" can prove deadly for your dog. The toxins in them will destroy your pup's liver cells, leading to often-fatal liver failure. Be aware of this when traveling with your dogs, too—especially to warmer climates where these plants are more likely to be found thriving outdoors.

## 43 From paw to mouth: Ice & snow melters can wreak havoc on your pup

If your pup licks enough rock salt or ice melt from their paws, you're both likely to be in for a long night. This licking can lead to digestive upset resulting in vomiting and diarrhea, and in high enough quantities, ice melts can also lead to seizures and other nervous system signs of salt poisoning. If you know that your sidewalks or roads have been treated, be sure to thoroughly rinse off your dog's paws after your walk and consider protecting their paws with a sturdy set of dog booties. Around your home you should also opt for one of the pet-safer* ice melts that are widely available. Your other pet-owning neighbors (and your plants) will appreciate it, too!

*No ice melters are truly pet-safe. Those that contain urea, glycols, or other non-salt components are certainly safer, though they can still cause problems if eaten in large enough quantities.

## 44 It's not a hit and run, it's a hit and cry

Sadly, every year many dogs are inadvertently run over in their driveway by those who love them the most—their owners. This is particularly common with older dogs who may not hear as well or be able to move as spryly as they once did—especially when they're basking in the sun. Get in the habit of giving a quick look under and around your car and then, pull out slowly.

Baxter an 11-year-old Golden Retriever, got slower in his later years and also liked to take longer and deeper naps. It was during one of these naps, on a warm summer day, that his owner backed over him as he pulled out of the garage and down the driveway. The damage to Baxter's chest was severe and, despite his owner's willingness and ability to spend whatever it took, sadly, Baxter succumbed to his injuries shortly after arriving at the ER.

# CHAPTER 2 BONUS ONLINE CONTENT

*Enter **tip#** below at PreventiveVet.com/Book-Extras to access this information.*

**LIST FOR HOUSEGUESTS:** Download a printable, customizable list to display for visitors so they can easily follow your "house rules." (#22)

**SETTING UP A DOG CRATE:** How to choose one, the safest set-up, and how to get your dog to love spending time in it. (#23)

**TRAIN YOUR DOG TO STOP COUNTER SURFING:** Videos and how-to tips to curb or prevent this behavior. (#25)

**COUNTER SURFING & STARTING FIRES:** See video of pets accidentally starting kitchen fires and what you can do to prevent it. (#25)

**WHAT TO DO IF YOUR DOG EATS YOUR MEDS:** Steps to take before you go to the Animal ER. (#26)

**NO MORE DOOR-DARTING:** Video and tips to prevent or correct this very common behavior. (#32)

**TOXIC PLANT LIST:** Find out what indoor and outdoor plants your dog should avoid. (#37)

**POISONOUS MUSHROOMS:** See photos of toxic mushrooms and tips on how to get rid of them in your yard. (#41)

**ICE MELTERS:** See which brands are pet-safer. (#43)

**BOOK EXTRAS**

# Safety When Out & About

## 45 Reconsider that retractable leash

Retractable leashes may seem like a good idea … more freedom, easier to store … so, what's not to love? Plenty. There are *many* drawbacks and dangers with using them—both for your dog (neck injuries, cuts to their legs, for example) and for you (eye injuries, cuts, rope burns, etc.). And if you ever drop the hard plastic handle, your dog is likely to spook and bolt, running into traffic or disappearing altogether. A sturdy, fixed-length leash isn't just a far safer option, it's also better for training your dog to walk well, because retractable leashes can actually *encourage* pulling.

Taxi a 3-year-old sheepdog, tested the limits of his retractable leash—and his owner's reflexes—when he bolted towards a much-loved neighbor on the other side of the street. His owner couldn't "lock" the leash in time and Taxi was off! Luckily it was a bike speeding by, not a car. The biker was able to avoid Taxi, but not the cord of his leash! Taxi suffered a minor neck injury and "road rash." His owner and the biker weren't so lucky though. The biker suffered a broken collarbone, while Taxi's owner dislocated his shoulder and broke three ribs when he was pulled to the ground. Taxi is now only walked on a 6-foot fixed-leash (attached to a "no-pull" harness, to decrease pressure on his neck that was injured in the accident).

## 46 Choke and pinch collars: There are better options

These types of collars should ideally never be used. They can cause, or worsen, certain neck and breathing problems for your dog, as well as causing serious injuries to other dogs they play with … and even you! These types of collars are painful and truly aren't necessary to achieve control. If it's control you need, work with a good, non-dominance theory-based trainer to help your pup with their "loose-leash walking" skills, and use aids such as head collars and no-pull harnesses instead.

## 47 Think twice before lettin' loose

Can your dog be off-leash? Sure … sometimes … under certain circumstances, in the right places, after *lots* of training, and even then … with caution (and risk). While having some off-leash freedom can be fun and even beneficial for dogs, there are a lot of risks not only to your dog, but to other dogs, people, and wildlife, as well. And that's even if your dog is "friendly" or well trained. Without a doubt, you should 100% definitely train your dog to be safely off-leash. (Tip: Start indoors and *really* nail their "stops," "check ins," and recall! See Book Extras for details.) But even then, exercise caution and good judgment before "releasing your hound." Everyone will be happier and safer for it.

## 48 Control without pain: Harnesses and head collars

Too few dog owners are aware of the availability of "no pull" type harnesses and head collars. Not only are these both more humane than their archaic "cousins"—prong collars and choke chains— they're also highly effective loose-leash walking aids. Harnesses keep pressure off of your dog's neck and trachea (windpipe), which can be hugely important in dogs (even puppies) of certain breeds or with existing neck or tracheal problems. Head collars also give you a quicker and more reliable method to prevent your inquisitive pup from eating something dangerous off the ground while on your walks (spoiled food, poisonous mushrooms, rat poisons, xylitol gum, and much more). This additional control and peace-of-mind is truly a wonderful thing—as is the fact that you won't be hurting your dog to achieve it!

# 49

## #HotHappensFast— avoid heat stroke

Heat stroke is a debilitating and easily avoidable emergency. It causes lots of suffering and is often fatal. Heat stroke happens frequently (but by no means exclusively) to dogs left in parked cars and those exercised too vigorously on hot days. Over-heating is particularly common in brachycephalic (short-nosed) dogs and their mixes, such as Bulldogs, Boxers, Shih Tzus, etc. It's also more likely to happen in dogs with certain medical conditions—including arthritis, obesity, collapsing trachea, and others. And because of their limited ability to regulate their body temperature, puppies and senior dogs are also at increased risk. Under the right conditions, heat stroke can happen in as little as 10 minutes! Check out Book Extras for more stats and tips on protecting your dog from heat stroke. And ever wonder what you can (and should) do if you see a dog left in a hot car? Head over to PreventiveVet.com/hot-happens-fast for a step-by-step guide.

**Sadie** a 7-year-old Standard Poodle, was rushed to the Animal ER after she collapsed from heat stroke in her owner's car. The windows were cracked while her owners ran into the store, and she was left with a bowl of water, but it was an unseasonably warm day in the low 80s. Despite very aggressive treatments and support, Sadie's blood clotting system failed. Her prognosis was grave, and Sadie's family had to make the heart-wrenching decision to euthanize her. Sadie was alone in the car for 20 minutes.

## 50 Does your dog need sunscreen?

Just as we can, our dogs can get skin cancer and/or sunburn from prolonged or repeated exposure to the sun. Fortunately, they can also benefit from sunscreen (with some cautions) and even UV-blocking clothing. When choosing a sunscreen for your pup, avoid those that contain PABA, salicylates, or zinc oxide. The areas on their body where most dogs are at the highest risk of sun damage typically include their ears, their nose/muzzle, and their belly (especially those that like to lounge on their back in the sun). Dogs that sleep near sunny windows indoors are also at risk, as UVA radiation can pass through glass!

## 51 Owie. Owie. Owie.

Remember the time you walked barefoot on the beach and had to hop towel to towel, or put your shoes back on because of the hot sand? Well, your pup's paws are at the same risk when walking on the sand (and even roads or sidewalks) on hot days. These surfaces can heat up quickly, and in some cases can even retain enough heat to burn your dog's paws long after the sun has gone down. If you can't comfortably hold the back of your hand against a surface for 7 seconds, then it's likely also too hot for your dog's paws. Avoid these surfaces on hot days, or protect your pup's paws with sturdy dog booties or protective socks if they must be out and about.

## 52 Make your dog glow in the dark

Thousands of dogs are hit by cars each year, even while on-leash. It's tough for drivers to avoid hitting what they can't see. Using reflective or self-illuminating collars, leashes, and clothing on walks with your dog between dusk and dawn, and especially when rain or other factors make visibility even worse, will help ensure that both you and your dog are seen and remain safe.

## 53   A dog park is not a place to 'tune-out'

Not every dog in a dog park is well-behaved. That's why it's important to know dog body language and pay attention to how your dog and others are interacting. If you see any concerning signs—leave. You'll avoid injuries, uncomfortable confrontations with other dog owners, and a few other problems. To learn about dog body language and how to handle "situations" at the dog park, check out Book Extras.

## 54 Communal water bowls: Think before they drink

Come summertime, "community" dog bowls abound outside of pet-friendly businesses and in dog parks. While these readily available water sources can be a great idea to keep out-and-about dogs hydrated and cool, if a sick dog drinks from them and it's not cleaned properly, or if your dog has a compromised immune system (young puppy, senior dog, or on chemo or steroids) communal water bowls can actually increase your dog's risk of illness (e.g., Giardia, Parvo, dog flu, and others). Help your pup beat the heat and stay safe and healthy at the same time by always bringing their own water supply, or carrying a good (collapsible) bowl or cup that you can fill yourself.

## 55 Sticks aren't free toys

Many dogs have been impaled in their chest, mouth, and even their eyes by the very stick they're playing fetch with. Unfortunately, some of these dogs do not survive their injuries. Plenty of dogs have also had to undergo anesthesia and tooth extractions for fragments that have become lodged between their teeth or embedded under their gums, while playing with or chewing sticks. Though sticks are plentiful and (initially) free, there are plenty of (relatively) inexpensive and far safer chew and fetch toys available.

### 56 The grass isn't always 'greener'

"Foxtails" and other grass seed awns are designed to burrow into the dirt, but they'll just as easily burrow into your dog's skin, eyes, ears, nose, lungs, and even their "swimsuit areas." If your pup is sneezing, shaking their head, squinting or limping after a run through a field of tall grass or even a walk around the neighborhood, bring them to your vet to see if it might be a foxtail. Left untreated, foxtails can cause painful and expensive problems. If foxtails are unavoidable, get your pup a mesh head guard and a good pair of dog booties. And always, always, check them thoroughly for foxtails after walks through or near tall grass.

### 57 Be(e) aware of bees and wasps

Visit any Animal ER mid-spring through mid-fall and you'll likely see lots of dogs with swollen faces and bumps all over their bodies. Most of these dogs will have tried to eat or otherwise tussle with a bee, wasp, or yellow jacket, and while their swollen faces can look super cute and pitiful (they really do!), it's actually quite dangerous. Allergic reactions to these flying insects can be mild and just cause a few hives and some itchiness, but they can also lead to swelling around their airways, causing breathing difficulties, and even anaphylaxis, resulting in shock, collapse, and death. Check out Book Extras for info on preventing these nasty stings, as well as what to have in your first-aid kit just in case. (Note: a dog's reaction to stings can get worse the more times they get stung!)

## 58 Curbs: Take a step back

Ever notice the tire marks on curbs at some intersections? It takes just one person cutting their turn too tight to injure or kill your pup if you're standing too close to the street. Pay attention and wait with your pup a couple of steps back to prevent a heartbreaking accident. The milliseconds you save by being closer to the curb are nowhere near as important as the life you'll save by being further back.

## 59 Escalators are NOT dog-friendly

If you take your dog on an escalator or moving sidewalk they should always be in your arms for the entire trip. If they're too big to be in your arms, or if your hands are too full, find another way to get between floors. Escalators and moving sidewalks can and have caused painful and disfiguring injuries to dogs who have been unfortunate enough to get their paws, ears, or leashes caught in the end plate teeth. Carry or avoid—always!

# 60 Rat & mouse poisons—at home, around town, and on the road

These compounds are designed to kill, and they don't discriminate between your dog and the rodents you're targeting. There are many types available, and the toxicity of some can be significantly worse, and more difficult to treat, than others. Research thoroughly, follow all label instructions to the letter, and be extremely careful where you store and use these poisons. Some reputable exterminators use pet-safer methods of rodent control or you can try nature's rodenticide … a cat (or a terrier)!

City parks, schools, restaurants, hotels/motels, and vacation rental homes are common places these poisons may be used. Also, when moving into a new apartment or house always ask if rodenticides are in use, and make removal of them a condition of any rental or purchase agreement.

**Maggie** a 3-year-old Dachshund, was brought to the Animal ER because of difficulty breathing. The problem started two days before—after a late-night, off-leash walk with her owner around a city park. It was determined that the breathing difficulties were a result of the blood that had built up in her lungs from the rat poison she had eaten while in that park. Thanks to vitamin K replacement, oxygen supplementation, blood transfusions, and other intensive care, she's okay. However, her treatment cost her family almost $5,000 and a lot of distress. Maggie's status was touch-and-go and she had to be away from her family and littermate brother for four days. Following Maggie's brush with death, her owners became strong believers in the importance of keeping her on-leash.

## 61   Why your dog should steer clear of colored water

Does your dog like to swim or frolic in the water? Have you heard of "red tides"? What about blue-green algae? If you and your pup plan to spend any time near lakes, ponds, reservoirs, (slow flowing) rivers, or oceans, you should 100% be aware of these Harmful Algal Blooms (HABs) and learn to recognize and avoid them. HABs occur for a variety of reasons and can be present in both salt and fresh water. These dog-dangerous water conditions are becoming more common and can seriously sicken, or even kill a dog. (And they aren't good for you, either!) HABs can result in everything from mild skin irritation to liver failure, seizures, and death. HAB toxins cause problems when a dog eats (typically dead) fish from the contaminated waters, or even just from a dog coming into contact with the water. And in bad red tides, the algal toxins are highly concentrated in the sea foam and can even be present in the air! Keep an eye out for posted warning signs, though they aren't always there. So check out the interactive map and other resources in Book Extras online to learn when and where HABs are most common in your state, as well as what they may look like.

## 62   Rip currents are dangerous—for people and dogs!

Warning signs for these deadly currents will often be posted on beaches with lifeguards. However, not all beaches are guarded and not all rip currents are marked. "Rips," as they're called, can occur on the beach of any large body of water with breaking waves—including lakes. Not only have dogs drowned in rip currents, but so too have distraught owners who've jumped in trying to save their struggling dog. To learn how to identify a rip current, and what to do if you or your dog is caught in one, check out Book Extras.

## 63 Snake, rattle, and roll

If you live or routinely hike with your pooch in an area where rattlesnakes are common, or are traveling to an area they might inhabit, look into avoidance training. You can also discuss the use of the rattlesnake vaccine with your veterinarian, as it may buy you a little more time in the event of a bite.

A rattlesnake bite is a serious and debilitating emergency. The venom's toxin is painful and can prove rapidly fatal. If your dog is bitten—vaccinated or not—an immediate trip to the veterinarian is of the utmost importance.

## 64 'Kissing this prince' doesn't have a fairytale ending!

When "kissed," a Bufo toad (aka cane toad) definitely won't turn into a prince! When threatened, these giant toads release a highly toxic milky substance from the glands around their neck. If your pup gives this toad even a single lick, it could be deadly. Find out if Bufo toads are present in your town or in areas where you plan to travel or hike with your pup. If your dog does get a lick in, immediately wipe their tongue and gums with a dry cloth and then, with their mouth pointed downwards to prevent swallowing of the water, rinse their mouth out with water from a hose for 10 to 15 minutes. Then call a veterinarian or animal poison control to get further advice. If there is any staggering, drooling, vocalizing, collapse, or convulsions, bring your dog to the vet immediately.

*Jessie* a 7-year-old dachshund, got sprayed by a skunk in his yard early one morning when his mom let him out to pee. It was right by the garbage cans! Mom saw the skunk, but Jessie didn't respond to her calls for him to "come." He eventually came scampering back, stinking of skunk. She threw him in the bath to rinse him off and used tomato juice to "de-stink" him. After a few dousings, she rinsed and toweled him off and set about her day. Unfortunately, Jessie kept squinting and dragging his face across the carpet. (He also still smelled of skunk!) Mom took him into their vet where they determined that the skunk spray must have gotten into and irritated his eyes. They checked for corneal ulcers (there weren't any), flushed out his eyes and sent him home with pain medications, eye drops, and an E-collar. They also gave Mom a better "de-skunking" recipe using peroxide, baking soda, and dish soap! (Mixture proportions in online Book Extras, if you ever need it yourself!)

## 65 Travel anxiety and carsickness

Unfortunately, many dogs develop (or already have) travel anxiety, which doesn't just affect their quality of life, but will likely affect yours, as well. And it may even increase your risk of being involved in a car accident! Help your dog by getting them comfortable in the car and during travel. Create positive associations by playing games with them or feeding them treats or meals in the car (while it's parked, not while it's moving, of course!). There are also some calming aids that can help, including certain supplements, anti-anxiety clothing, dog pheromones, and even medications. Whatever you do, don't let your pup ride on your lap to calm them down when you're driving … that puts you and EVERYONE else on the road at risk.

## 66 Wind through their fur—cute, but dangerous

Letting your pup ride in the car with their head out the window makes for cute photo opportunities and they may be loving it, but it just isn't safe. Not only can kicked-up rocks and other flying road debris injure their eyes, ears, nose, throat, or skull, but one sudden stop or a passing squirrel can send them bolting out into oncoming traffic. It's okay to open the windows a bit, but not enough for your pup to get their head out—even if they're wearing eye protection (doggie goggles).

## 67 Buckle up pup for the drive

Be it a crate, carrier, or travel harness, proper dog travel restraint won't just keep your pup safe, it'll do the same for you, your family, and everyone else on the road, too. Restraint decreases your dog's risk of injury or death in an accident or sudden stop; decreases your chances of being distracted by your dog and causing an accident in the first place; and also prevents your pup from jumping through an open window or rifling through the contents of your bags while your eyes are focused on the road. Safely restraining your pup is easy to do—especially if you start from an early age. There are several good and effective options available. The key is to choose a product that has been properly tested and to use it correctly—for every trip, no matter how short and no matter how calm your pup may seem to be in the car (or truck bed)!

**Scotch** a Labrador Retriever, was 4 years old when he jumped out of an open window in the family car as it sat at a stop sign only three blocks from home. The family didn't see the squirrel he was likely chasing, but they did see the passing car that hit him as he ran through the intersection. Scotch suffered brain swelling, multiple rib fractures, and internal bleeding as a result of his accident. He did survive, but needed a full eight days in the ICU. Scotch now wears a travel harness every time he goes for a ride, no matter how short or long the trip.

# CHAPTER 3 BONUS ONLINE CONTENT

*Enter **tip#** below at PreventiveVet.com/Book-Extras to access this information.*

**RETRACTABLE LEASHES—USEFUL OR HARMFUL?:**
See the many reasons these are dangerous tools and when you might be able to use them. (#45)

**WHAT'S WRONG WITH THE PRONG:** SF-SPCA busts prong collar myths. (#46)

**CHECK-INS:** Video and how-to tips to train your dog to "check-in" (look at you voluntarily) on- and off-leash. (#47)

**HOW TO HELP A DOG YOU FIND IN A HOT CAR:**
Step-by-step list of what to do, from when to contact the authorities, to how to document the situation, and how to help the dog with heat stroke. (#49)

**HOW TO AVOID SUNBURN RISK:** Tips and products to protect your pup from sunburn and skin cancer. (#50)

**AVOID NIGHTMARES:** See how you can easily help your dog be seen at night and walk safely. (#52)

**HOW TO BREAK UP A DOG FIGHT SAFELY:**
Video tips on what to do. (#53)

# CHAPTER 3 BONUS ONLINE CONTENT

*Enter **tip#** below at PreventiveVet.com/Book-Extras to access this information.*

## MOTHER NATURE MAKES LOUSY DOG TOYS:
Check out our safer fetch "stick" (and get an exclusive discount!). **(#55)**

## FIND OUT WHICH RODENTICIDES ARE BEST TO USE:
See which products are safer for pets. **(#60)**

## HABS MAPS: Check out your state's map for alerts on
where HABs (Harmful Algal Blooms) are located. **(#61)**

## RIP CURRENTS: Learn what they look like and what to do
if your dog is caught in one. **(#62)**

## TEACH 'STAY AT A DISTANCE': Watch videos that
show you how to train your dog to stay and sit on the spot
(out of danger). **(#63)**

## CAR TROUBLES: Tools and tips that can help or prevent travel
anxiety and carsickness In dogs. **(#65)**

## TRAVEL RESTRAINT: Car harnesses, booster seats, crates, and
more. Find out which are safest and what to look for. **(#67)**

**BOOK EXTRAS**

Go to **PreventiveVet.com/Book-Extras**, enter this code: **3HS-T2F6-8D** to unlock this resource

# Preventive Vet

## CHAPTER 4

# Overall Health
# & Wellness

## 68 Minimize or avoid vet visit stress

We vets recognize that visiting us can be stressful or anxiety-inducing for some pets. We try to make the experience as pleasant and calming as possible, but you can help your pup as well, by acclimating them to your vet's office. One way is with regular "social visits." These are all about sniffs, snuggles, and treats, and can go a long way towards helping to prevent or reduce current and future visit stress. Many practices encourage them, you don't even need an appointment, and they're free! This is just one way you can help, and there are many other tips and techniques in Book Extras—far too many to list here. Check them out, especially if you have an anxious dog.

## 69 Yearly check-ups are about so much more than just 'shots'

Visits to the vet aren't just about vaccines—in fact, they're often not about vaccines at all! You know your dog best, but just because your dog looks healthy to you, doesn't necessarily mean that they are. Dogs are masters at hiding pain and disease—doing so would've helped them survive in the wild. Fortunately for them (and you), we vets are experts at detecting problems. The importance of a good vet exam cannot be overstated. Abdominal organ enlargement, heart murmurs, and abnormalities within your dog's eyes are just a few of the long list of things that your vet checks for during a physical exam. Prevention, picking up on concerning trends, and early detection of problems are so important for a long, healthy, happy life for your pup.

## 70 Learn how to check these 3 important vital signs

Knowing how to check your dog's temperature, pulse, and breathing (respiratory) rate, as well as knowing what is normal for them, can help you determine when there is a problem that might require first aid or a trip to the vet. Typical "normal ranges" vary based on your pup's age, size, breed, and several other factors—but how to check them doesn't. Ask your veterinarian or one of the nurses to show you how to check your pup's vital signs. You don't need to check them often, but you should know what's normal for your dog, so you can better recognize when something is "off."

## 71 Oral health = Overall health

Imagine the state of your mouth if you never brushed your teeth or had them cleaned! And it's not just the teeth that suffer from poor oral care, it's also the kidneys, heart, and other organs. Introducing your pup to having their teeth brushed early on, can make their oral care easier for life. Good dental health can be achieved with toothbrushing, certain treats or diets (VOHC* approved), and regular dental exams and cleanings with your veterinarian. Ask your vet for a brushing demonstration. Note: don't use toothpaste made for people! Xylitol (Tip #9), fluoride, and foaming agents can all cause problems for your dog.

*Note: When looking for dental treats, chews, foods, and even toothpastes, talk to your veterinarian and look for the VOHC Seal of Acceptance. The Veterinary Oral Health Council (VOHC) evaluates the studies companies do to determine their validity and helps to ensure that their products will actually "do what they say on the tin."

## 72 Protect your pup throughout their life with appropriate and timely vaccines

While dogs don't need *every* vaccine *every year,* vaccines are critically important—especially for puppies who need to complete a series of vaccines to be fully protected.  Vaccines are about the health and well-being of your dog, as well as that of all the other dogs in your community. And in the case of some vaccines—such as leptospirosis and rabies—immunizing your dog protects you, your family, and your neighbors, as well. Many factors go into determining the best vaccination plan for an individual dog—including age, where in the country your dog lives and travels to, current outbreaks, how "social" the dog will be and what activities they will do, as well as a host of others. Work with your vet to determine which vaccines will help your dog, and when and how often they should have them.

## 73 The worms that will break your heart

Hopefully you've heard of heartworms by now. But are you aware of how dogs get them? (Answer: Bite from an infected mosquito.) Or where they live in a dog's body? (Answer: In their heart, but also in their major blood vessels.) Or whether or not they're a problem where you live? (Answer: They've been diagnosed in all 50 states and cases are growing, so odds are good that they are!) Or just how absolutely devastating heartworms can be? (Answer: Heartworm disease is absolutely devastating! As in serious debilitation, heart failure, and death.) Treatment of heartworm infections in dogs is possible (but it isn't without its risks, and it can be quite costly). Thankfully, there are great heartworm preventative medications available from your veterinarian. There are also some simple steps you can take to keep mosquitos out of your yard and home, check out Book Extras for more on those.

## 74 Parasite prevention: Doing it safely and effectively

Mosquito bites transmit heartworms to dogs, and far too many dogs are sickened by or die from heartworm disease every year. Other parasites such as fleas, ticks, and some common intestinal worms, which cause disease in dogs, can also cause disease in people. All of this is preventable, but the key is consistent, year-round use of effective preventatives on all of your pets (including indoor-only dogs and cats). There are many choices of preventatives and some are better (and safer) than others for your specific dog (age, where you live, other pets in your home, etc.). Your veterinarian is truly your best resource for figuring out a safe and effective parasite prevention program, so be sure to ask and take advantage of their expertise.

## 75 What is your dog at increased risk of?

Some medical conditions and illnesses are more likely to occur in certain breeds; these are known as breed predispositions. In some cases, prior knowledge of these predispositions can help you reduce their effects or even prevent them entirely. There are DNA tests that can tell you your dog's breed(s), as well as tests that can screen for common genetic conditions that may affect your dog. They're not always perfect, but with a little bit of research and a conversation with your veterinarian you may be able to uncover steps you can take to prevent or otherwise spare your puppy discomfort and illness (and save you time, money, and heartbreak in the long run, too).

*Note: It isn't just your dog's breed that can affect their risk for different issues. Certain illnesses, poisonings, traumas, and other problems can be more likely in dogs that spend time doing different activities (hiking, Frisbee, hunting, etc.), go to different places (groomer, daycare, boarding), or live with people who are diabetic, have young children, or are smokers, for example. Discuss your dog's activities, lifestyle, and living situation with your vet to see what steps you can take to minimize health and safety risks.*

## 76 'Bloat' can affect all dogs, but some breeds are more at-risk than others

Technically called Gastric Dilatation and Volvulus (GDV), "bloat" is a painful, serious, and rapidly fatal emergency condition. Treatment typically has a high success rate, but quick recognition on your part and an immediate trip to a veterinarian are crucial. All breeds and mixes are susceptible to this condition. However, certain breeds are at increased risk—including Great Danes, Doberman Pinschers, Setters, and other deep-chested breeds—especially if they come from a breeding line with a history of GDV. Several other factors can increase your dog's risk, too (e.g., fast eaters). Talk to your vet about your dog's risk for developing GDV, and, if the risk is deemed high, consider having the preventive surgery done. Called a gastropexy, it can be done at the time of your dog's spay or neuter, or any time. For additional information and tips to prevent and recognize bloat, see Book Extras.

## 77 'Fast food': What to feed in a pinch

If you ever run out of your dog's food and can't get a new bag of it in time for their next meal, don't just grab any random bag of dog food off the store shelf (even if the ingredients look similar). Sudden food changes are a sure recipe for digestive upset for your pooch. Spare your dog the pain— and your carpets the stain—by picking up a pack of boneless, skinless chicken breast and a bag of white rice from the market instead. Boil both and combine in a 50:50 ratio. This is a great non-irritating, "bland diet" stand-in for the day or two that it might take to get a new bag of your dog's regular food. To avoid this situation, try portioning out one week's worth of your dog's regular food each time you get a new bag. Set that amount aside, and when you open that "backup bag" you're reminded that it's time to go shopping.

## 78 Need to change foods? Avoid 'cold turkey.'

While variety may be the spice of your life, for your dog it can often lead to digestive upset. If you decide to change your pup's diet, be sure to do so gradually, ideally over 1 to 2 weeks. Increase the new food by 20–25% every 3 to 4 days until you've completely transitioned to their new food. By slowly decreasing the percentage of their old food while simultaneously increasing the amount of the new, you provide a chance for their digestive enzymes and gut bacteria to adapt to the new diet, minimizing and sparing them uncomfortable and distressing bouts of vomiting and diarrhea.

## 79 Portly pooches are unhealthy (and uncomfortable)

Obesity in dogs has become very common. Like in humans, obesity puts dogs at increased risk for a variety of health problems—arthritis, high blood pressure, heart disease, skin infections, and many others. It also increases the risk for certain emergencies, like cruciate ligament tears, heat stroke, and severe pancreatitis. Dogs (typically) don't feed themselves and very few will truly self-regulate if given a full bowl. So, if you measure or weigh their food carefully—even a few extra kibbles here or there can add up to a lot of extra calories (especially in a small dog)—you can help your pup get to and stay at a healthy (and comfortable) weight. And keep in mind, too, that treats are often a huge factor! The general rule of thumb for treats: keep them (well) under 10% of your dog's daily calories.

## 80 Puppy socialization: Crucial for a well-adapted, happy dog

The first three months of your puppy's life are the most crucial for their social development. During this period it's important to (safely and responsibly) get your pup comfortable with a variety of people (e.g., children, people with beards, in wheelchairs, and of different ethnicities), sights (e.g., balloons, traffic, horses, bikes), sounds (e.g., vacuum cleaner, sirens, baby cries), and surfaces (e.g., linoleum, concrete, grass, carpet). Doing this will help prevent a host of behavioral problems later in life. All hope is not lost if you don't get your dog socialized in the 3-month window, but it may take more time and patience on your part.

Socialization includes things you can do at home, around your neighborhood, and in organized puppy socialization classes. But it's not only about exposing them to things; it's also important that they have a positive experience and are comfortable with those things, too. How and when you introduce them to new people and experiences is very important.

When socialization involves places frequented by other dogs, such as dog parks, your vet should guide the timing of it. In most cases, socialization with other puppies, in a controlled and clean environment, can start shortly after their 8-week-old vet visit and vaccinations. For important information and additional tips on puppy socialization, check out Book Extras.

## 81 When your dog thinks the sky is falling

Many dogs have or develop a fear of fireworks, thunderstorms, and other loud noises. Should your dog ever develop such fears, be sure to speak with your veterinarian about medications and other options that can help them cope. Better still, help your pup avoid this problem by acclimating or desensitizing them to these unavoidable noises early on in life. There are specialized anti-anxiety jackets, and musical resources, as well as other calming aids and techniques that can help. A small investment of time and money now will pay off as decreased stress and improved quality of life for both you and your dog in the long run.

## 82 Can't we all just get along?

Introducing a new dog to the pets already in your home may take some doing, but doing it right can help to ensure long-term harmony and can help prevent injuries and stress, too. For introducing a new pup to an established dog, have their first meeting be on "neutral territory" (i.e., take them both for a long walk together). When it's an established cat you'll be introducing your new dog to, bring your pup for a long walk or play session to get rid of some of their energy, then keep your dog under good leash control upon entering the house and making them available for your cat's inspection. And be sure to take a second to trim your cat's nails before doing any introductions—your dog's eyes will thank you for it! When introducing your new dog to any established pets, it's crucially important to go slowly and to do so in "small doses." Never force or rush the issue on either pet, always be present to observe and monitor, and always speak in a calm, praising voice—and use plenty of love and treats.

## 83 The right trainer is worth their weight in gold!

This small, early investment will pay off in many aspects of your pup's overall health, safety, and happiness, and will make your life far easier in the long run. The type of trainer you choose can either enhance or undermine your relationship with your dog. Force-free trainers are best, as they focus on positive reinforcement (R+), desensitization, counter-conditioning, and other methods that help build a collaborative bond with your dog. Avoid those who profess and practice dominance (alpha-dog) theory.

## 84 Leave no ear, tooth, or paw untouched

It's important, from Day 1, to get your pup accustomed to you touching and evaluating their teeth, ears, and paws. Not only will this make your at-home, routine care easier, it will also greatly reduce the stress your pup may experience in your vet's office and at the groomer. As an added bonus, it will help you detect problems earlier and may make the treatment of those problems easier and less expensive.

## 85 Regular baths and brushings make for a happier, healthier dog

Some basic grooming will not only keep your dog's coat clean and free of mats and certain parasites, but it will help you with early detection of wounds, swellings, and potentially cancerous growths. Brushing and combing also helps decrease stress—for both you and your pup. The recommended frequency of bathing and grooming can vary between breeds, time of year, and lifestyle factors, and too much bathing, or bathing with the wrong type of shampoo, can lead to dry, irritated skin. So, talk with your veterinarian, breeder, or your groomer to learn what frequency and products are best for your dog.

## 86 Reach for the clippers, not the scissors

Dogs frequently get mats and "stuff" stuck in their coat. It's often hard to know where a mat, wad of gum, tree sap, or other sticky material ends and your pup's skin begins. To avoid cutting your dog's skin (and causing a surprisingly concerning level of bleeding), step away from the scissors and opt for an electric beard trimmer instead. These trimmers are far safer and typically do a better job anyway. Alternatively, bring your dog to your veterinarian or a groomer to have the offending material removed. Any of these options will be less likely to result in a painful, bloody cut, and an emotionally (and physically) scarred dog.

## 87 Ear infections: Now hear this!

Ear infections are consistently among the top reasons people bring their dogs to the veterinarian. Sadly, they often do so only after an infection is well established and has already caused their dog significant discomfort. A quick weekly look and sniff will spare your pup discomfort and save you time and money. Ask your vet, or one of the nurses, to show you how to safely clean your pup's ears. Then clean and dry them as needed—especially following any swimming or baths where water is more likely to get into your dog's ear canals and cause irritation and infection.

And speaking of baths and your dog's ears, never dump a cup or pitcher of water over their head to rinse and never spray their head with the shower nozzle or an outdoor hose. Regardless of how careful you think you might be, you're certain to get some water down the ear canal, setting up the perfect warm, moist environment where ear-infection-causing yeast and bacteria will thrive! Rather, always wash and rinse their head with just a damp washcloth or sponge.

## 88 When NOT to clean your dog's ears

It's not always a good idea to just jump in and start cleaning your dog's smelly or infected ears. Of course you want to help, but there are actually times when you can do more harm than good, causing them more pain and suffering, or potentially even deafness! These times could include when your dog has something stuck down in their ear canal that you can't see (like a foxtail—Tip #56), when their eardrum is ruptured, or even when their ear is already red, raw, and painful. If your dog is really digging at or dragging their ear (along the floor or furniture); if they've suddenly become "head shy" and pull away when their ear is touched; if the inside of their ear flap is already red, dry, cracked, or bleeding; or if your pup is doing any abnormal circling or tilting of their head, bring them to your vet before diving in with an ear cleaner or administering any "leftover" medications you may have. This is the best way to help your dog, and to avoid a very unfortunate situation.

**Junebug** a 5-year-old German Shorthaired Pointer, unintentionally sent her mom to the (human) ER one day after seriously biting her hand. Junebug's mom noticed that she had been shaking her head and scratching at her ear for the past couple of days, so she decided to give her ear a good cleaning. Unfortunately, (for both of them), Junebug's ear was already raw and painful from the foxtail that had found its way down into her ear canal. While her mom and dad headed to the (human) ER, their son brought Junebug to the vet. They sedated her, removed the offending foxtail, and applied a medication that addressed her ear pain and the infection that had formed in her ear. (Fortunately Junebug's rabies vaccination was up-to-date, so her mom didn't have to worry about getting shots herself, and her hand also healed without permanent nerve damage.)

## 89 Keep those nails short

It's important to keep your pup's nails well-trimmed. Long nails can catch on things, causing them to rip and bleed (a lot)*. Long nails can even grow into your dog's feet and paw pads, causing pain and infections. And, if that isn't enough, long nails can make walking painful for your dog and can scratch up your home flooring. Ask the team at your vet's office or your groomer to show you how to safely cut (or grind!) your dog's nails, or just let them do it for you. If cared for regularly and properly, you shouldn't hear their nails click on the floor when they walk.

*Note: If they've got them, don't forget about your dog's dewclaws (their "thumbs"). Because they don't really ever come into contact with the ground, they don't wear down naturally. They are the nails that most often get caught on something and tear, and they can bleed a lot! They're also common nails to overgrow into the skin and nail bed, so don't forget to trim them.

## 90 A pinch of cornstarch can help in a pinch

Proper nail care is important for your pup's health and comfort. But should you ever cut too short (which many people, even professionals, have done), you'll want to have something on hand to stop the bleeding that's likely to occur. You can get styptic powder at any pet supply store, but if you ever catch yourself without it, a pinch of cornstarch will work just as well. Just press and hold a little bit of cornstarch onto the tip of the bleeding nail for a few minutes and all should be good.

## 91 Use safe collars and tags—or let them go naked (sometimes)

What may seem like a trivial decision (choosing a collar or dog tag), is actually far more important than that. When your dog is in a crate or on a deck, you should avoid using collars and dangling ID tags. Dogs have died from strangulation in their struggle to free themselves when the loop on their collar or their tags got caught between deck slats or the wires of their crate. Breakaway-type collars and ID tags that lie flat against your pup's collar can help prevent this. You could also let them "go naked" (i.e., no collar) in these situations … just make sure they're microchipped if they'll be outside without their collar/tags.

**Reggie** an 8-month-old Rottweiler, was sleeping soundly on his family's deck one day when the ID tag hanging from his collar got caught between the boards of the deck. His mom came running from the other room when she heard his yelps and panic on the deck. Thankfully, she acted quickly enough to unbuckle his collar, freeing him and preventing his strangulation. Soon thereafter, Reggie's mom got him microchipped and Reggie now "goes naked" in the house, while in his crate, and, of course, when on the deck.

## 92 Fitbit for dogs—not just a fad!

Awesome step-counting, vitals-monitoring, GPS-enabled "wearables" aren't just for people. There's a whole range of "smart-collars" for dogs! Could your dog benefit from one? It's certainly possible and, even if not now, they may benefit from one in the future. Since wearable collars can monitor and track everything from location and activity level to pulse and respiratory rates, and even temperature, they can actually have some serious health benefits for portly pooches, those with arthritis, dogs with epilepsy, and a host of other medical conditions. With this tech in place, you may even be able to detect a problem before it starts, or at least catch it earlier once it does. Some wearables can even be used to monitor responses to medical treatments or recovery following surgery.

## 93 Microchips reunite families and save lives

Having your dog microchipped is a simple, yet important step that can help reunite you with your dog should they get lost or stolen. They are important even if your dog wears an ID tag, as those can fall off. You can have your dog "chipped" when they are getting spayed or neutered, or at any other time. Be sure to register the chip, keep your contact information up to date, and have your veterinarian scan and check the chip at your dog's wellness check-up each year to make sure it still functions properly.

## 94 Would you go to your dentist to fix your broken arm?

You wouldn't, right? Well, your dog needn't either. Veterinary medicine has come a long way since the days of your first childhood pet! One of those ways is the availability of veterinary specialists (internists, oncologists, dermatologists, and many others). Know that if your dog ever develops a complicated, stubborn, or recurrent problem, your veterinarian may recommend referral to one of these specialists. While it may appear to cost more at first, you may get to a diagnosis and appropriate treatment earlier, saving you time and money in the long run and sparing your dog additional discomfort.

## 95 Accidents happen—be prepared, and know your limitations

Not every accident or emergency is preventable and knowing what type of first aid to do (and what not to do) can have a big impact on your dog's comfort and survival. In cases such as bee stings (Tip #57), poisoning, choking, heat stroke (Tip #49), and many others, this is very important information to have. Check with your local Animal ER or humane society to see if they offer first-aid classes. But note that first aid is often just that: *first* aid. Meaning that, in many cases, a veterinarian should still see your dog after you've provided initial care.

**Mr. Beans** a 5-year-old Airedale Terrier, got into a bit of a scuffle at the dog park one day, leaving him with a couple "little bite marks" on his back. His mom took him home, got out her first-aid kit, gave a little shave, and scrubbed the wounds. And Mr. Beans was back to good! But he wasn't really. Four days later, Mr. Beans was brought into the ER because of a lack of energy and appetite, and trouble breathing. What his mom didn't realize when she was doing her first aid, was that one of the bite wounds from the dog park scuffle was more extensive than she thought and had actually penetrated into the chest cavity. The bacteria from the other dog's tooth wreaked havoc in Mr. Beans' chest, establishing a nasty infection ("pyothorax") that was the cause of his lethargy and breathing troubles. Thankfully Mr. Beans made a complete recovery with chest tube placement and intensive care, but it took five days and several thousands of dollars to get him truly back to good. While Mr. Beans' mom's first aid was a good start, it wasn't all the care he needed on that first day. She now realizes that.

## 96 Pet first aid tools—at home and on the road

Just as knowing appropriate first aid is important, so too is having the tools to properly administer it. A good pet first aid kit is an important investment for both your home and vehicle. Many stores and online sites sell them, or you can easily put one together yourself. Start with the list in Book Extras, but talk to your veterinarian about their recommended items for your kit, and if there should be any specific additions based on your dog's breed, lifestyle, or existing medical conditions.

An accurate pet first aid manual can be handy for treating minor injuries and illnesses at home, and It can also be useful for knowing when it's time to seek professional medical help. Keep it by your first aid kit so you can easily find it when needed. There are also some great pet first aid apps for tablets and phones, allowing you to have this important information close at hand.

## 97 Spaying and neutering: It's not just about pet overpopulation

You're likely aware that spaying or neutering your pup will prevent unintended pregnancies. But what you may not know is it can also tame undesirable behaviors (like running out of your yard in search of "love"), prevent disease (certain cancers), and ease the treatment of some chronic conditions (epilepsy and diabetes). Speak with your veterinarian about the procedure and when would be the best time to have it done. Even for breeding dogs, this is an important procedure once their breeding days are behind them, as it can help prevent certain emergencies (such as uterine infection or urinary obstruction) and other health problems.

## 98 Post-Op: Follow doctor's orders—even if you think your dog is feeling better

Following any surgery, including a spay or neuter, your pup (or even you) may not be too happy about having their exercise and play limited. But returning to these activities too soon—going to the dog park or even just running around in your home—or removing an E-collar (that dreaded cone!) prematurely, can delay healing and result in complications such as infection or bleeding. These can land your pup back on the surgery table, prolong their recovery, and cost you additional time, money, and stress. When scheduling any surgery for your dog, ask about post-surgical home care so that you can best prepare yourself and your home for what will be needed during your dog's recovery.

## 99 'Stoic' to their own detriment

Sadly, it isn't just bones* that dogs are good at hiding. They can also be masters at hiding pain. While this "instinct" may have served them well back in their pre-domesticated days, it can lead to prolonged suffering and otherwise avoidable worsening of problems in this day and age. To best help your pup stay healthy and comfortable, recognize that they won't always show you blatantly obvious signs of pain. Painful pancreatitis? They may just show you a little more sleepiness, slightly less interest in food, and a bit of a hunched back. Agonizing arthritis? Maybe just a "bit slower getting up," or not as willing to jump on or off the couch is all you'll see. Get to know what's normal for your dog and then pay attention to and seek veterinary care for even the subtle signs. Knowing how to check your dog's "vital signs" (Tip #70), and maybe even a "smart collar" (Tip #92), can also help you "see past their stoicness."

*Don't forget ... dogs shouldn't have bones (Tip #6).

## 100 Don't play doctor— even if you are one!

"Safe for people," even for babies, does not equal "safe for dogs" and many people—including "people doctors" and nurses— have unintentionally poisoned, sickened, and even killed their own dog by self-prescribing. Medications and supplements should be given to your pup only on the advice of a veterinarian. Even if you are a human pharmacist, medical doctor, or nurse, you should follow this tip, as the pharmacodynamics and pharmacokinetics of certain drugs vary significantly between species.

## 101 Video strange behaviors

How good are you at charades? Strange question, right? Well, it's not as strange as you might look or feel when you're acting out your pup's hacking, shaking, collapsing, snorting, or whatever behavior is bringing you to your vet's office. While we in the profession promise to never judge your acting skills (OK, maybe "never" is too strong a word), we'd honestly rather see your pet doing their "strange" behavior themselves. And since they frequently won't do it when in the exam room, the next best thing is to video the behavior at home and bring it along to your appointment. If you still want to show off your charade skills, by all means have at it. We "promise" not to laugh.

*Have fun, and may you and your dog enjoy many happy, healthy years together!*

# CHAPTER 4 BONUS ONLINE CONTENT

*Enter tip# below at PreventiveVet.com/Book-Extras to access this information.*

**VET VISIT DE-STRESSERS:** Tips to prevent or remove fear and anxiety from your dog's vet visits. **(#68)**

**DOGGIE VITAL SIGNS:** Video how-tos for checking pulse, temperature, and other dog vitals. **(#70)**

**DENTAL PRODUCTS THAT PASS THE VOHC SEAL OF APPROVAL:** See a list of dental and oral health products that are confirmed to perform "as advertised." **(#71)**

**WHAT YOUR PUP CAN EXPLORE & WHEN:** See which vaccines open up new adventures for your pup. **(#72)**

**MOSQUITO REPELLANTS:** Keep insects off and away from your dog safely. **(#73)**

**HOW TO RECOGNIZE BLOAT (GDV) EARLY TO SAVE YOUR DOG:** See an important video of a dog bloating (it's not graphic and he survives!). **(#76)**

**HOW MANY TREATS ARE TOO MANY:** We provide a calculator to help you figure it out. **(#79)**

**100+ SOCIALIZATION IDEAS:** Download a checklist of sights, sounds, and other stuff to introduce your new dog to. **(#80)**

**SHAMPOO FOR DOGS:** Find out which kinds NOT to use. **(#85)**

**FIRST-AID KIT ESSENTIALS:** Check out a list of products to put together a kit for home and on the road. **(#96)**

**BOOK EXTRAS**

Go to **PreventiveVet.com/Book-Extras**, enter this code: **3HS-T2F6-8D** to unlock this resource

Preventive Vet

# CHAPTER 5

BONUS TIPS

# Preparing for Emergencies

# AT THE END OF THE DAY, YOU CAN'T PREVENT EVERYTHING.

Trust us, we've tried, it can't be done! Accidents will happen—there's a reason they're called "accidents." Do your best to recognize and be aware of the dangers in your pup's environment and become familiar with the signs of a problem. Try to be prepared and to know what to do (and not to do), but—very importantly—don't be too hard on yourself. Even when you practice prevention something could "slip through." You're only human and dogs will, after all, be dogs. In the event of a problem, your veterinarian, pet poison control hotline, and your local Animal ER are your best resources and they're there to help.

## 1 Keep important phone numbers on speed dial

Whether at home or while traveling, having the phone numbers for your veterinarian, the closest Animal ER and a pet poison control hotline programmed into your cell phone can save you time, money, and stress. And it may well save your pup's life! Also, make sure to provide these to your dog sitter when you leave your pup in their care.

## 2 It's 11 p.m., do you know where your closest Animal ER is?

In some pet emergencies, time can truly be of the essence. Knowing the location of your nearest Animal ER, both at home and when you travel with your dog, can save your dog's life and minimize your stress. Don't forget to leave this information with those caring for your dog while you're away, too.

### 3 Emergency planning —include your dog

If disaster strikes and evacuation is necessary, you certainly don't want to leave your dog behind. You also can't afford to spend precious time scrambling to figure out who's leashing up the dogs, or where the travel crates and first-aid kits are. Create an evacuation plan that includes your pets, and make sure you have a place to go that will accept them. It'll decrease stress and improve everyone's chance of survival.

### 4 Financial aid for the unexpected

If an emergency or illness strikes before you've signed your dog up for pet insurance, or you just don't have enough room on your credit card, know that there are some third-party financing options available. Since most veterinary hospitals don't offer payment plans, these resources can help to soften the initial financial blow of unexpected medical costs. Just be sure to read the fine print and make the required minimum payments or you'll be slapped with penalties and a surprisingly high interest rate.

## 5 Consider pet medical insurance—sooner rather than later

The costs of veterinary care, especially for treatments resulting from emergencies or chronic illnesses, can be quite high. Luckily, nowadays, pets can benefit from many of the same life-saving treatments that humans do, and similarly the bills often run well into the thousands of dollars. These costs increase even more with veterinary specialists, such as oncologists or dermatologists. Having a good insurance policy—particularly for emergencies and illnesses—can give you peace of mind and protect you from having to base important decisions about your dog's medical care solely on finances. There are many important things to look out for when choosing a pet insurance policy, so talk to your veterinarian and do your research. Since no policy covers pre-existing conditions, you should buy it *before* you need it.

Felix a 2-year-old Chihuahua, was attacked by a larger dog while playing at the dog park. He suffered bite wounds to his chest and abdominal cavities, requiring extensive surgeries, chest tubes, and prolonged care in the Animal ICU. He recovered fully, though now he only goes to dog parks with separate "small dog" areas. His owners were thankful that they never had to think twice about the significant costs for the life-saving care Felix required—they had signed him up for pet insurance shortly after his first puppy visit to their vet.

# INDEX

# INDEX

# INDEX

## 'TAILS' OF WOE

# 101 ESSENTIAL TIPS BOOK SERIES

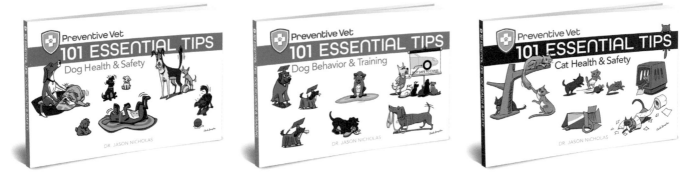

**Enjoying your book?** Our entire *101 Essential Tips* series is designed to provide the awareness and advice you need to help your pets live their longest, healthiest, and happiest lives. If you'd like to buy another book from the series, for yourself or a fellow pet lover, you can visit *PreventiveVet.com/101-series*. There's an exclusive offer waiting for you.

# ABOUT THE AUTHOR

Dr. Jason Nicholas—"Dr. J"—is The Preventive Vet. Providing pet owners with awareness and knowledge that can help them keep their pets happy, healthy and safe is his passion and his calling. He created Preventive Vet in 2011 to ensure that pet owners everywhere would have reliable information, advice, and the tools they need to enjoy the best lives together with their pets.

As one of the foremost experts and public speakers on health and safety for cats and dogs, Dr. J travels far and wide to raise awareness about pet illness and emergency prevention. He is an author, media resource, and a general practice and emergency veterinarian who is happiest when helping pets and their people.

Dr. J graduated with honors from The Royal Veterinary College in London, England, and completed his Internship at the Animal Medical Center in New York City. He and his family (both two-legged and four) are now lucky enough to call the beautiful Pacific Northwest their home.

## Paws & Play
### WITH DR. J

*Preventive education on the go!*

Subscribe to our newsletter and podcast for more tips and awareness for living a longer, safer life with your pets.
*PreventiveVet.com/PawsAndPlay*

 iHeart RADIO

 Listen on Apple Podcasts

GET IT ON Google Play

LISTEN ON STITCHER

# NOTES

## Welcome to the Preventive Vet world... where pets are protected and celebrated!

We're not just about helping you avoid pet hazards and dangers, we also love celebrating the relationships between pets and their people and the many joys that pets bring to the world. So come join us and other pet lovers on our website and social pages. Interact, get more tips, and share your stories. You can even post a pic of your pup enjoying their *101 Tips* book!

## *Sniff around and check us out!*

 PreventiveVet.com

 instagram.com/PreventiveVet

 fb.com/PreventiveVet

 pinterest.com/PreventiveVet

 @PreventiveVet

 youtube.com/PreventiveVet

Did you enjoy and learn something new from this book? Do you think other dog lovers would benefit from this book? Please take a moment and give us a review. PreventiveVet.com/Book-Review